This book belongs to

Published by Fat Dog Publishing in 2017

First edition; First printing